THE
MAGIC
OF
WORDS

ARTHUR ALEXANDER

illustrated by R. S. Alexander

Prentice-Hall, Inc.,

THE
MAGIC
OF
WORDS

Englewood Cliffs, N. J.

another book by the same author: *The Hidden You*
illustrated by Zenowij Onyshkewych

Eleventh printing.......January, 1970

The Magic of Words, by Arthur Alexander

Library of Congress Catalog Card Number: 62-16651
Printed in the United States of America
54523-J (T)

to

ARTHUR FORBES ALEXANDER

who knew how to use words lovingly

CONTENTS

THE
MAGIC
OF
WORDS

THE WORD FOREST

What you are doing, right now, is almost unbeliev-able. You are making sense out of strange, black marks printed in a book. You are sharing thoughts with a person you can neither hear nor see. You have mastered the *word* puzzle. You are able to read.

Think with me for a minute. Think of a world without words! Could you *think* without words? Try it.

There was a time, of course, when you knew no words. When you were a baby about the best you could do to get a message across to anyone was to cry. When you were hungry you cried. If something frightened you or hurt you, you cried. But you couldn't tell anyone *what* hurt you or frightened you . . . at least not in words.

Think of how much of your life depends on your knowing how to use words: how making sense out of what other people say or write affects your life.

But make no mistake. Just because we use words every day does not mean that we know everything there is to know about them. After all, we don't expect to understand everything there is to know about a forest, just because we know what trees and bushes are.

Language, you see, is rather like a forest. A forest has many different kinds of trees and bushes. But, unless we can tell one from another, that's about all we know: a forest is just a lot of trees and bushes of different shapes and sizes. Oh, we might know what some of them are. Over there is a maple tree. And that is a huckleberry bush. Right in front of us we recognize a pine tree. But the rest of the forest seems to be just just a mass of green.

Well, they might be just trees and bushes *to us*. But to an expert they tell a fantastic story. They tell a story that may go back millions of years. A botanist, who knows about growing plants, can tell whether or not a tree is native to the part of the country in which it is growing. He can tell what family of bushes a particular bush belongs to. He may know how long a certain tree has been growing in the world. In fact there seems to be no end to the number of things an expert can see in a forest.

Now what about our "word forest"? Words may seem to be "just words" to us. But to a word-scientist, or *linguist*, words are more—much more. They, too, tell a fantastic story. A story that goes back beyond the time when there was such a thing as history: to pre-historic times. That's what *prehistoric* means: the time in the world before there were words that could be written down.

Our word forest includes the different "word families" that we call languages. Then there are all the relatives of words: numbers, signs, symbols, codes, and pictures.

As so often happens, there is one word that we can use for the work all of these things do. That word is *communication*. Communication stands for all the ways that men use to get across a message of some kind to each other.

As you will see later, men have communicated and do communicate in many different ways. They talk, write, make books, send smoke signals, use codes, draw pictures, send signals that are invisible for a while and then either make sounds or pictures—and even make both sounds and pictures.

How did it all begin?

How on earth can we make sense of all these things?

How did you learn to make sense out of strange sounds and marks?

Let's try to find out. For it is this ability to communicate and to think with words and their relatives that has made it possible for men to do the wonderful things they do.

One day a man by the name of Albert Einstein wrote down a message:

$$E = MC^2$$

It looks like a small message. Actually it is a very large message. And it is a very difficult message. It is so difficult that only a few people in the world really understood it at first. Yet this message helped men to understand atomic power in a way that has led to the marvels of this "Atomic Age." That's how powerful a simple-looking message can be.

TWO

IGPAY ATINLAY

If you have ever been with a dog for any length of time, you know that he can "tell" you quite a number of things. He can whine to let you know that he is unhappy about something. If a cat crosses his path, he may yap in such a way that you will understand that he is not altogether fond of the cat family. A stranger coming near the dog will hear loud barks and growls that warn him to "beware of trespassing." If you are a special friend of the dog, he will greet you with happy barks and movements.

In other words, the dog has a *kind* of language. So do other animals. Animals can let each other know how they *feel* at the moment. If we know the animal well enough, we can understand what he is "saying," too.

So, you may say, animals have a language that they speak, too. Man is not the only being that can communicate. And you are right. But there is a big difference!

Man makes use of sounds, marks, and gestures to get across *ideas* as well as feelings. Along with your ability to use your hands in so many ways, it is this that makes you superior to all the animals.

Lucky for us! For we are inferior to animals in many ways. We can not see nearly as well as an eagle or a hawk can. These birds of prey have more than three times as many "seeing cells" in their eyes as men have. Many kinds of animals have a better sense of smell than man. Our friend the dog can hear sounds the human ear is never aware of. The tiny bee picks up light waves with its eyes that our eyes never detect. In fact, it is possible that if men had had to depend on their senses, mankind might be extinct today.

The scientific name for man is *homo sapiens*. It means "man the wise." And one of the reasons we can be so boastful is the skill we have with languages.

You can tell a friend, for instance, what you plan to do *tomorrow*. You are able to say what you did *yesterday*. There is quite a difference between using language that way and using it to let a friend know simply that you are angry, or hungry, or pleased about something, isn't there?

In man's kind of language sounds, markings, and gestures stand for feelings, things, and ideas. Let's take our friend the dog again. "Dog" stands for a certain family of animals. But we could just as well use *Hund*, as the Germans do; or *chien* if we prefer French; or *perro* if we like to speak Spanish. *Dog, Hund, chien, perro;* each of these words are symbols for the barking creature we call "man's best friend."

Then, we know there are many different kinds of dogs. We may be talking about a *collie*, or a *dachshund*, or a *spaniel*, or a *beagle*. And each of these words or symbols lets our listener know what kind of a dog it is we are talking about.

But suppose we want to let someone know that it is just one special dog that we are talking about. We mention the dog by *name*. Our collie is not any old collie, but Lassy; our dachshund is Rudi; our spaniel answers to Checkers; and our baying friend, the beagle, is Bugle Ann. By picking certain names for our dogs, we can often let people know whether they are male or female. And then, of course, we have a special name for a dog if it is a baby. We call it a *puppy.*

Of course, none of this I have been telling you about words could be true if men hadn't agreed that these words do stand for one special thing, idea, or feeling. That's why people sometimes repeat the lines from Shakespeare's *Romeo and Juliet:* "What's in a name? That which we call a rose by any other name would smell as sweet."

So you see it doesn't have to be any particular symbol. As long as people agree that the symbol has a special meaning, it can be any kind of word.

One more thing about these word symbols we use. Right now you are probably reading quietly to yourself. That means you are looking at some marks printed in a book and these marks are getting a message across to you.

Now read aloud. They aren't just marks in a book when you read aloud. They seem to stand for certain sounds you can make with your voice. Words can be either sounds or marks. And men have to agree on the sounds just as they must agree on the marks.

Take the German word for dog again: *Hund.* If you

pronounce that word as if it were an English word, chances are you would say it as if it rhymed with "sunned." Germans would not. They would say it as if it were spelled *hoont.*

Think now of animal sounds: the barks, growls, and whines of the dog, for instance. Not quite the same thing as our word sounds, are they?

"Oday ouyay ikelay iceway reamcay?"

Do you understand that message? It is in "Pig Latin." Many boys and girls have used this "language" to speak to each other. It may sound quite foreign when you hear it spoken. But it is really plain old English with a different sound given to the words. To speak Pig Latin, take the first letter from the beginning of the word, put it at the end of the word, and add the sound "ay" to it. In Pig Latin "you" is *ouyay.* If the word happens to begin with a vowel (*a, e, i, o, u,*), leave the word as it is and tag a "way" to the end of it. In Pig Latin, "old" would be *oldway.*

If you and a friend agree to speak Pig Latin to each other, and you both know how it works, you will understand each other even if it doesn't sound like English. Your *agreement* on the meaning of sounds make this possible. In fact, this idea of a group of people agreeing on the meaning of signs or sounds makes all kinds of codes and other "secret languages" possible.

THREE

SECRET WRITING

Have you ever wanted to send a secret message to someone? If you have, the first problem you had to solve was how the person could get the message you wanted to send without anyone else catching on to the secret. Whether you wrote the message down or spoke it or made certain sounds, the message had to have meaning to you and to the person you were sending the message to—and to no one else.

The answer to your problem of sending a secret message is to send it in *cryptography*. This word comes from two Greek words put together, *kryptos* (hidden) and *graphein* (to write). This word, cryptography, covers the many forms of secret messages.

Probably the earliest method of sending secret messages was *code*. If a mother and a father want to say something to each other that they don't want their child to understand, they will probably use a code. Spelling out the word instead of saying them could be a code. Spelling the message will work out fine for parents as long as the child has not yet learned how to spell. They might, for instance, spell out this message:

L-E-T-S G-I-V-E J-U-N-I-O-R A T-R-A-I-N F-O-R

H-I-S B-I-R-T-H-D-A-Y

By *spelling* the message, mother and father have used a code that Junior can't understand. If they had said the message in regular words, Junior would have known what they were talking about. And there would have been no secret. Mother and father can go on using this code until Junior has gone far enough in school to know how to spell. When that has happened, they will have to find a new code to use if they want to send secret messages within Junior's hearing.

One of the best known forms of code is known as *cant.* Cant is a secret language made out of regular words. In very early times it was used by gangs of thieves and other criminals. The famous French "poet-thief," François Villon, who was born in 1431, used cant in many of his wonderful poems.

Criminals are not the only people who use cant. Recently a cant was made by people who came to be called *beatniks.* Some of these cant words were *cool* (meaning anything liked, or approved of by a beatnik), *pad* (for the place the beatnik lived in), and *square* (for any person who was not a beatnik).

Another interesting cant is used by Cockneys (people born in London's East Side). A Cockney will use words that rhyme with the actual word he means: *twist and twirl* means "girl," *storm and strife* is a "wife," and *north and south* stands for "mouth." You can have fun with your friends by making up some "Cockney cant."

Of the many different codes, the best known is the Morse Code. Samuel Morse, the inventor of the telegraph, sent his code messages by turning an electric current off and on. A short release of electric current through a telegraph wire made a *DIT* sound. A longer flow of electric current made a longer sound: *DAH*. By combining these *dits* and *dahs* (or dots and dashes) messages could be sent by telegraph, and later by radio.

But before real messages could be sent, the *dits* and *dahs* had to be given some kind of meaning. Here is the meaning these sounds were given:

A · —	H · · · ·	O — — —	V · · · —
B — · · ·	I · ·	P · — — ·	W · — —
C — · — ·	J · — — —	Q — — · —	X — · · —
D — · ·	K — · —	R · — ·	Y — · — —
E ·	L · — · ·	S · · ·	Z — — · ·
F · · — ·	M — —	T —	
G — — ·	N — ·	U · · —	

You don't really have to use a radio or a telegraph to "send" the Morse Code. You can whistle it, tap it, use an electric buzzer or bell, or think up some special way of sending it that is all your own. See if you can read this message in Morse Code:

— · — · — — — — · · · · · · · — · — · · · · — · · · — — · ·

Another form of cryptography is called *cipher*. Cipher is a method of secret writing that substitutes other markings for the letters of the alphabet that will give the actual message. The "code" part of the Morse Code are certain short forms of messages that are sent. SOS is such a message. In the International Code, SOS ($\cdots --- \cdots$) stands for the message: "I am in danger and need immediate help." Many people have thought SOS was an abbreviation for "save our ship" or "sink or swim." This is not so. It is a code signal only, not an abbreviation.

We can use cipher by making use of another alphabet in which to write our message. Let's borrow some marks that were used by the ancient Phoenicians and Greeks in their alphabets. We will pretend that these marks stand for English letters in our cipher:

Now, can you read this message in our cipher? In other words, can you *decipher* this message:

There is one other main form of secret writing, in addition to code and cipher. This form is called *concealment*. Concealment, of course, means hiding. In this form of cryptography, the message has to be hidden from the view of people who are not supposed to see the message.

One simple way to send this kind of secret message is to write a short message on the outside of an envelope, then stick the postage stamp over the message. Other seals or stickers could be used for this purpose.

During World War II, the Germans printed a message they wanted to send to their secret agents. Then they took a photograph of the message. Finally they reduced the negative of the photograph to such a small size that it could be placed over a period dot in an innocent-looking typewritten letter.

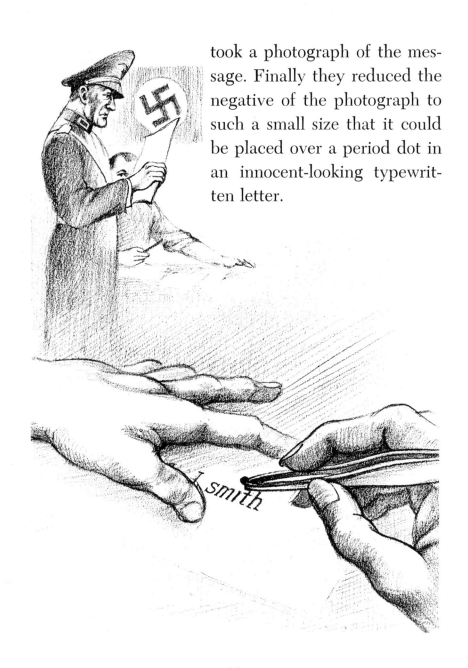

The agents who were to receive this secret message had been told to lift the tiny negative off the period dot, enlarge it, and read the message. Unfortunately for the Germans, American agents got hold of the message first and discovered the trick.

Another way to send a hidden message is to use *invisible inks*. These invisible inks are liquids that are colorless and, therefore, invisible on white paper. When the paper is treated in some way (by heating it, for example) the liquid will darken so that the message can be read clearly. Such things as certain fruit juices, milk, and baking soda in water may be used.

The best way to hide your message when you use invisible ink is to write between the lines of an innocent-looking letter. If you would like to see how this works, try this:

Take some milk. Use a clean pen nib in a holder. Use the milk as you would regular ink, and print your message on fairly heavy paper, or on a card. Let your message dry.

Now place the paper or card on a hot steam radiator, or a hot electric light bulb, or a warm iron. When the paper or card gets hot, you will be amazed to see your message gradually appear—clearly written in what looks to be brown ink.

FOUR

"BOW-WOW"
OR "POOH-POOH"?

How on earth did one human being ever think of making a sound that would tell something to another person? How, in other words, did *talking* ever begin? For that matter, how did you ever begin the whole complicated business of being able to talk, speak, write, read, and listen?

Frankly, no one—not even language scientists—can give a full answer to any of these questions. But there are some theories (theories are rather like wise guesses).

Some of the theories of how language began have rather funny names. One of these is the "bow-wow" theory. This theory of how language began says that man began to use words that imitated the sounds he heard in nature. A man, the "bow-wow" theory claims, would hear a dog barking. The dog's bark sounded like "bow-wow" to the man. The word the man would choose for this animal that barked would then be *bow-wow*.

One of the main troubles with the "bow-wow" theory is that people who speak different languages seem to hear the same natural noises in different ways. In English, we say a bog darks *bow-wow*. A Frenchman, however, says a dog goes *oua-oua* when he barks. Italian dogs, or so it seems to Italians, bark *bu-bu*. And, while we say a rooster goes *cock-a-doodle-doo*, Italians hear it as *chicchirichi* and Frenchmen, as *cocorico*.

Then we have the "pooh-pooh" theory of the beginning of language. This says that in the beginning stages, language was made up of the sounds we seem to make almost naturally when we are surprised, hurt, pleased, fearful, and so on. Thus, when we are amazed at some-

thing we might see, we say *wow!* If we are hurt, we might say *ow!*

The "yo-he-ho" theory is rather like the "pooh-pooh" theory. This one says that language began with the sounds human beings make when they are working hard. Thus, if a group of men pull and shove a heavy object, they might grunt *yo-he-ho.*

Along with the "yo-he-ho" theory, there is the belief that early men sung sounds, much the way babies do, over and over again. These sounds gradually took on meaning, the theory says. This is called the "sing-song" theory.

But, no matter how many theories there are for how language began (and we have talked about only a few here), the great mystery is still unsolved. Will it some day be solved? Many word scientists think not. The trouble is, they say, that when men began to talk, they left nothing that a scientist today could examine. The scientific study of the beginning of language can begin only with written language. And, the scientists say, man began speaking some tens of thousands of years before he began writing!

Of course, scientists today do study how language begins with each of us. They observe the ways a baby learns to talk. One theory that has come from this is the "babble-luck" theory. You have probably heard a baby babbling at some time or other. The "babble-luck" theory says that the baby babbles and babbles when he reaches a certain period of growing. Then one day by "luck" he babbles a sound that is like a real word. Junior might be babbling "da-da-da-da," when his proud father hears him.

"Well, what do you know?" says the proud father. "Junior is saying *daddy*. He is talking at last!"

Then father smiles at Junior, repeating "daddy" several times and pointing at himself. Junior, it is said, slowly gets the idea that the sound, *da-da*, has something to do with the big creature he sees from time to time around the house.

There have been cases where human children have been lost, and were said to grow up with animals: wolves, monkeys, dogs, and so on. And if you have read Kipling's, *The Jungle Book,* you know the story

of Mowgli, the boy who grew up with the wolf family. In *The Jungle Book*, you may get the idea that human children can talk in a human kind of language to animals. This is not true. In real-life stories of children who lived for a long time with animals, the wild children, when they were found, had not developed a human kind of language on their own. What noises they made were simple grunts, growls, squeals—and similar animal-like noises.

But—and this is an important difference between animals and man—many of the wild children were able to learn a human language after they had been with men for a length of time. This is something their animal "parents" and friends could not do, no matter how long they heard men talk.

Some people have thought that by studying the sounds made by animals, a clue to the beginnings of man's language could be found. Chimpanzees have been watched carefully, and the sounds they make have been recorded for close study.

About sixty years ago, a man by the name of Garner claimed that chimpanzee sounds and the sounds of other members of the ape family made up a language. He claimed that he had been able to learn some of these sounds and had had "conversations" with the chimps. Other language scientists have said that this is impossible. In a book called *The Great Apes,* however, Robert M. Yerkes says that the chimpanzee might be trained in the use of a *sign language.*

In recent years the clever porpoise has been the subject of a great deal of study by scientists. The porpoise has a large brain, and some scientists believe that this brain may be as remarkable as the human brain.

Dr. John J. Dreher, a language scientist, has noted the large number of clicks, sputters, and whistles a porpoise

makes. He was able to pick out eighteen different kinds of whistles from all the sounds the porpoises made. Although Dr. Dreher believes that many of the sounds are used to help the porpoise (by echoes) find his way through the seas and for food, many of the whistles may be used as a kind of language.

Of the eighteen different whistles Dr. Dreher has heard, twelve of them fell into a pattern in terms of how often they were used.

This is very much like the pattern of words most often used in human speech.

Although the study of animal speech may not help us to find out how man began to talk, it is a fascinating subject. Perhaps someday you may be able to talk to a porpoise!

RANK	CONTOUR
1 ...	⌣
2 ...	⌣
3 ...	⌒
4 ...	∿
5 ...	⋀
6 ...	⌇
7 ...	⋀∿
8 ...	⌒
9 ...	∿
10 ...	⋁∿
11 ...	⌣
12 ...	⌣

FIVE

WORDS AND MAGIC

It is April Fool's Day. A boy has made up a story to fool a friend on this special day. There is not a word of truth in the story. The boy who is telling the story has his hands behind his back. If we sneak around behind the boy and look at his hands, we will see that he has crossed his fingers. You can guess why.

Have you ever blown out the candles on a birthday cake? What did you do just before you blew the candles out? Did you make a wish? If you made a wish, did you keep it to yourself because you believed if you *told* your wish, it wouldn't come true?

Have you ever "knocked on wood" after you said something? Perhaps you might have said, "I haven't had to miss a club meeting all year—*knock on wood!*"

Boys and girls (and grownups, too) have been doing such odd things as these for a very long time. The reason they have been knocking on wood, crossing fingers, making secret wishes, and so on, lies in the belief that there is something magical about words.

Just think of all the stories you have heard or read that have something to do with guessing a name or a word. Usually the person who guesses the word has the power to break some kind of magical spell.

Do you know the story of Rumpelstiltskin? Do you remember how this evil dwarf's power was destroyed when his name was found out?

Stories about the magical power of words have probably been told as long as men have been telling stories to each other.

The idea of word-magic comes from the belief that a word and the thing it names are mysteriously connected. Long ago people believed that they had to stop an enemy from finding out their right name. Many men believed that if an enemy found out a name, he would be able to curse the owner of the name. Even today we find people repeating things that spring from this belief —even though the people using them do not know it. Have you ever heard other boys and girls saying something like this:

"What's your name?"

"Puddin' Tane! Ask me again and I'll tell you the same!"

Or perhaps you have heard someone say: "Aha! I've got *your* number!"

And who hasn't said or heard this:

"What's your number?"

"Cucumber!"

You will probably be able to think of other things you have said or heard that are like these sayings.

We don't really believe today, of course, that an enemy or an evil spirit will have power over you if he finds out your name. But sayings (such as the ones we have just talked about) that went with that belief in times past are still with us.

If we're honest with ourselves, perhaps we can even remember a time when we believed just a little bit in "word magic."

SIX

WRITING AND READING PICTURES

We have seen that *speaking* words began tens of thousands of years before *writing* words was thought of. Stories were not read, they were *heard*. Before the invention of writing, the only "books" were human books—men who told stories. These "human books" had to have very good memories.

Very few people have good enough memories to remember many details. In the days before writing if a man wanted to remember that he had lent someone a jug of wine, for example, he might draw a picture of it on the wall of his storeroom. The more men felt the need to remember things, the more they felt the need to have a way that would help them remember.

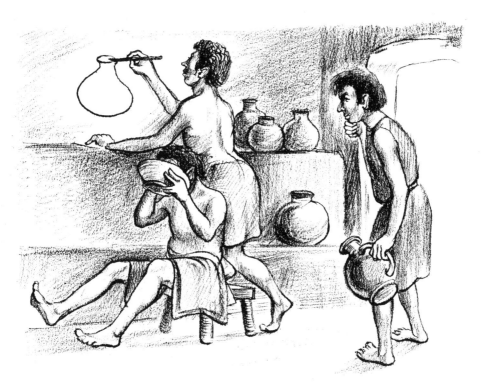

As we might guess, probably the first form of writing was *picture-writing*. If man wished to write "face," he would draw a picture of a face. If he wanted to write down "fish," he drew a fish. This kind of writing is called *pictographic* which means "picture-writing."

The real trouble with pictographic writing is that there are only so many things you can draw pictures of. You can't draw a picture of "truth," for instance, or of things like "bad," "good," or "bright." The early inventors of writing, however, were very clever. They soon learned to join pictures together to get over certain *ideas*. The early Chinese, for instance, joined their pictures of the "sun" and "moon" to form "bright."

Sun 日   Moon 月   Bright 日月

Linguists call this *ideographic* writing, which means, as you can guess, "idea-writing." The written Chinese language to this day is ideographic.

Now we come to a very interesting development in the history of writing. Some people began to make certain pictograms and ideograms stand for *sounds* that are made in spoken language. The Egyptians, for instance, did this.

To understand how this works, let us look at a *rebus*, a kind of picture-puzzle. Can you figure out what this rebus says:

If you guessed that it means "I would not believe Bill Lockhart," you are right. Notice that "believe" can be made by combining the pictures of the bee and the leaf. And Lockhart can be shown by the pictures of a lock and a heart.

The picture-writing of the ancient Egyptians is called *hieroglyphics.* Egyptian hieroglyphics worked very much the way a modern rebus does.

Lioness   Mouth   Snake   Bowl   Crane   Field

But clever as the Egyptian use of hieroglyphics was, it does not equal our modern alphabet. We owe the wonderful system of writing we have today to the *Phoenicians* and to the *Hebrews.* As you know, our system of writing allows us to write *any* word with only twenty-six signs: the letters from A to Z that we call the alphabet.

Our word *alphabet* tells us that this system of writing came originally from picture-writing. The word *alphabet* is made from putting together the Greek forms of the first two letters used by the Phoenicians and the Hebrews. *Aleph* meant "ox" and the letter that gradually came to be our "A" was at first the picture of an ox's head:

aleph   ox   A

Beth meant "house" and the first "B" was a picture of a house:

beth   house   B

45

The Greeks got their alphabet from the Phoenicians about 3,500 years ago. The *Etruscans*, in turn, based their alphabet on the Greek one. And, finally, the Romans made up their alphabet from the Etruscan. The Roman alphabet, with a few small changes, is the one we use today in English.

Another alphabet that is used by many people today is the *Cyrillic* alphabet. This alphabet is based on the Greek. The Cyrillic alphabet, with some added signs, is also used by the Russians, the Belorussians, the Ukrainians, the Bulgarians, the Macedonians, and the Serbs.

A strange alphabet was used in northern Europe (mainly by the Vikings) beginning about fifteen hundred years ago. It is called *runes* (rhymes with *moons*) and it means "a secret or a mystery." At that time very few people knew the meaning of the runes that were scratched on hard objects like trees, stones, and armor. Many people thought the runes had magic power.

So you see, just as spoken words had "magical power" for early people, so had alphabets.

It is an interesting fact that many of our modern English words tell us something about the history of writing—just as the word alphabet does. Take our word "write," for instance. Back in the early days of our language, this word meant "to scratch or cut." And, as we

Greek	Cyrillic	Roman	Contemporary
A	A	A	A
B	Б	B	B
Γ	В	C	C
Δ	Г	D	D
E	Д	E	E
Z	E	F	F
H	Ж	Z	G
Θ	З	H	H
I	И	I	I
K	I	J	J
Λ	K	K	K
M	Λ	L	L
N	M	M	M
Ξ	N	X	N
O	O	O	O
Π	П	P	P
P	Р	Q	Q
Σ	С	R	R
T	Т	S	S
Υ	У	T	T
Φ	Ж	U	U
X	Ж	V	V
Ψ	З	W	W
Ω		Y	X
			Y
			Z

have just seen, the runes were *scratched* or *cut* into hard objects. Our word "book" is one of the Old English words for "beech tree." Runes were often cut into beech trees. Even the word "read" has a connection with the runes. At one time this word had a meaning much like "decipher or guess." People had to "guess" or "decipher" the meaning of runes. Our word *paper,* by the way, comes from "papyrus," the writing material made by the Egyptians from reeds that grew along the Nile River.

At first glance, we may see no magic in words. But if we look closely, we will see that they breathe the magic of history—even the most ordinary, everyday words.

SEVEN

SOLVING LANGUAGE MYSTERIES

How do linguists decipher the meaning of "dead" languages that have not been used for thousands of years? To answer this question we must think back to what we talked about in the chapter on codes and ciphers.

We shall begin with a true story. In 1799, some French soldiers, commanded by Napoleon Bonaparte, were digging trenches near the city of Rosetta in Egypt. While they were digging, they came across an enormous black stone. On the stone was a message in three different languages: Greek, Egyptian hieroglyphics, and a later, easier form of Egyptian writing. Named for the city near which it was found, this stone is known today as the Rosetta Stone. It can be seen in the British Museum in London.

For a long time before the Rosetta Stone was un-
earthed, people had been trying to understand the
meaning of the ancient Egyptian hieroglyphics. But try
as they might, word-scientists had no luck in working
out enough of the meaning of the mysterious picture-
writing that had puzzled scholars for centuries.

50

In a way, the hunt for the meaning of the hieroglyphics was like the work of secret service men who try to break the codes and ciphers of enemy spies. The Rosetta Stone was to be the "key" that would break the code.

An Englishman, Dr. Thomas Young, knew from the work of other word-scientists that the names of Egyptian

kings and queens were given special attention in hieroglyphics. This was done by drawing a *cartouche* (an
oval ring) around the name. In this way the royal names
were given emphasis in much the same way that we
give emphasis to a word by putting a line under it.

Dr. Young had found out that one of the names on
the Rosetta Stone was Ptolemy V, one of the Greek
kings of Egypt. He found this out by comparing Egyptian hieroglyphics with the Greek writing on the stone.

Cleopatra   Ptolemy

Meanwhile, the name of Cleopatra was found on a
monument. Young was able to work this out with the
help of what he had learned from finding the name
Ptolemy. Now, let's look at the Greek forms of these two
names: PTOLEMAIOS and KLEOPATRA. Young
could guess that the first hieroglyphics in each name
had to stand for the sounds of "P" and "K." The second
then had to be "L" in *Kleopatra.* And Young found it in
the right spot in *Ptolemaios.* You notice that Kleopatra
has two A's; so Young knew that the hieroglyphic that
is repeated in that name had to stand for the sound of
"A." Working on in this way, Young was able to puzzle
out a few hieroglyphics.

The next person we meet in our mystery story of the Rosetta Stone is a young Frenchman by the name of Champollion. By picking out hieroglyphics he already knew, thinking out the meaning of others, and guessing once in a while, Champollion was finally able to decipher the hieroglyphic message on the Rosetta Stone.

If I tell you that # % * = means *stop*, can you figure out what = * % # means? Remembering what we know about ciphers, we can work that out fairly easily. It means *pots*, of course. This is a simple explanation of the way Champollion worked. Of course, his work was much, much more complicated. Picking up from where Champollion left off, other men were at last able to make a dictionary of hieroglyphic words.

Many language scientists believe that the Egyptians got the idea of writing from the Sumerians. These people lived in the Near East between the Tigris and the Euphrates rivers. The oldest writing that has so far been discovered was found in a Sumerian city, and dates back about five thousand years. The Sumerians used a system of writing called *cuneiform,* which means "wedge-shaped." It is so named because the signs used in this form of writing are shaped like wedges. This kind of writing was done on soft clay tablets with a sharpened reed that left wedge-like shapes.

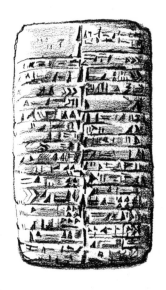

When the clay tablets with cuneiform writing were first discovered, no one could read them. In 1835, however, an Englishman named Rawlinson found a huge, very high rock at Behistun, in the country we now call Iran. Like the Rosetta Stone, the Behistun Rock had three different kinds of writing carved on it.

One column of the Behistun Rock carried cuneiform writing. A second was in an ancient language that was unknown. But the third column was written in an old form of Persian. Many word-scientists could read enough of the old Persian language to use it as a key to the meaning of the other two languages.

The writing on the Behistun Rock told of the victories in battle of a Persian king, Darius. Finally, after several linguists had read, puzzled, and studied for a long time, the mystery of cuneiform writing was solved.

Not all of the known ancient languages can be read yet. Only a few years ago another young Englishman, Michael Ventris, deciphered a language that had been a mystery ever since samples of it had been discovered. This was a language used by the people of ancient Mycenae in Greece. It is called *Linear Script B*.

Another undeciphered language, *Linear Script A*, used by the people of Crete in times past, may yet be read by using *Linear Script B* as a key.

EIGHT

HAND-TALK

If you want to get a message across to someone without making a sound or writing a word or drawing a picture, what do you do? The chances are you would make some kind of movement. You might put a finger to your lips if your message was: "Be quiet. Don't say a word or make a sound." You could agree with something that was said by moving your head up and down. Or you could say "no" to someone by moving your head back and forth sideways.

This shows us, then, that language can take the form of body movements or *gestures*. It is one way that people who speak different languages can "talk" to each other. You may ask someone, for instance, what time it is. His reply may be a shrug of the shoulders. You then understand that he doesn't know the time.

Most language scientists agree that "gesture language" was used by men long before spoken language. In other words, long before men talked with their mouths, they were talking with their hands.

"Well," you might say, "a person using gestures couldn't *say* very much." But that is not true. In fact, it is said that there are about seven hundred thousand different gestures that can be made. So, you see, it would be possible to have a complete language using just gestures.

The North American Indians did make use of gestures in a very important way. Almost everyone is familiar with Indian "sign language." Boy Scouts, particularly, have made a special study of this language of gestures.

In the days before the white man settled the Great Plains, many tribes roamed across its grassy flatlands. Each tribe spoke a language that was so different from another tribe's, that it was impossible for men from different tribes to speak to each other. The problem of communication was cleverly solved by the Plains Indians with the use of sign language. The gestures were simple, but they were able to get ideas across.

The Indian sign for "time," for instance, was to hold both hands out in front of the chest with the index fingers pointing ahead. The right hand would then be drawn back about two inches. By using the same sign for

"time," but drawing the right hand back several inches, an Indian could express the idea of "before," or "long time in the past." In the same way, "after" was made by making the sign for "time," then moving the right hand past and ahead of the left. This meant also "long time in the future" and "since."

This sign language of the Indians was a remarkable invention. Men from such tribes as the Arapaho, Kiowa, Sioux, Crow, and Cheyenne could meet together and discuss their problems in the same language—even though each of the tribes spoke a language as different from the others as French is from English. It was as if all the members of the United Nations could meet together and discuss their problems without the help of translators.

Sign language was a necessity for the Indians of the past. But, today it is used by boys and girls for fun. The International Boy Scout organization has adopted the Indian sign language. When Boy Scouts from as many as thirty-seven different nations meet at their Jamborees, they carry on their business and have private conversations in sign language.

The Boy Scouts are not the only group that is making use of sign language. Teachers who wanted to help people who are unable to hear or speak (*deaf mutes*) have trained their students in the use of sign language.

So skilled are many deaf mutes in this language that they can speak together at a very rapid rate.

The United States Navy has taken advantage of the sign language used by deaf mutes. At Gallaudet College for the Deaf, in Washington, D.C., navy frogmen study sign language so that they can communicate with each other when they are under water.

In a way, all of us who live in cities make use of a "language" that is really a sign language. We cross streets when we see green lights. A green light tells us: "It is safe to cross." We can tell whether an elevator is going up or down by various signs. We go in certain directions if signs with arrows point the way. How many different signs can you think of that give you messages?

NINE

NUMBERS, NOTES, AND NONSENSE

If you think about it, you will see that most of man's knowledge is tied up with his mastery of language. You will also see that language is not a simple thing. No one book, not even a very large book, could begin to tell the whole story of the magic of words.

Let's take a quick look at languages that do not use what we ordinarily think of as "words." We have seen that an entire language can be made of gestures. An entire language of a kind is made up of numbers, letters, and other signs. It is the language of mathematics.

Remember Einstein's formula: $E = MC^2$? That is a message written in the language of mathematics.

Probably you read messages that are written in a form like Einstein's every day you go to school, messages like $14 + 12 = 26$, or $9 \div 3 = 3$, or $3 \times 9 = 27$.

This language is one that all of us make use of in one way or another. And, in the way sign language was used by the Plains Indians, it can be understood by people all over the world—whether the language they speak is English, French, Russian, Japanese, or Swahili. It is a universal language.

There have been many different number systems, but the one we use now seems to work best for us. It is called the *Hindu-Arabic* system because it came to us from India, by way of the Arabs. As you know, it makes use of only ten *digits* or symbols: 0, 1, 2, 3, 4, 5, 6, 7, 8, 9. Yet with those ten digits we can form any number we want to. Incidentally, can you guess why many number systems are based on *ten?* Here's a hint: how many fingers (include thumbs, please) do you have? How many toes do you have? Our word *digit* comes from a Latin word meaning *fingers* or *toes*.

	1	2	3	4	5	6	7	8	9	0
Roman	I	II	III	IV	V	VI	VII	VIII	IX	X
Egyptian	I	II	III	IIII	IIIII	IIIIII	IIIIIII	IIIIIIII	IIIIIIIII	∩
Hindu-Arabic	1	2	3	8	4	6	7	8	9	0
Chinese	一	二	三	四	五	六	乂	八	九	十

Another kind of language is understood almost anywhere in the world. It is the language of musical notation. No matter what language he speaks, a pianist may look at a sheet of music and play the same sounds as the composer of the music intended him to play. Besides the notes, there are other signs in music that tell the musician many things, such as how loudly or softly to play, what speed to play at, what mood the music should have, and many other important messages.

Naturally, any language must be learned—whether it is a word, gesture, sign, number, or music language. And, once learned, a language should be used for its greatest possible effect: the clearest message it can possibly deliver. It may be a comic effect, such as

Lewis Carroll's use of "nonsense" words in "Jabber-wocky":

'Twas brillig, and the slithy toves
   Did gyre and gimble in the wabe:
All mimsy were the borogoves,
   And the mome raths outgrabe.

"Beware the Jabberwock, my son!
   The jaws that bite, the claws that catch!
Beware the Jubjub bird, and shun
   The frumious Bandersnatch!"

He took his vorpal sword in hand:
   Long time the manxome foe he sought—
So rested he by the Tumtum tree,
   And stood awhile in thought.

And, as in uffish thought he stood,
   The Jabberwock, with eyes of flame,
Came whiffling through the tulgey wood,
   And burbled as it came!

One, two! One, two! And through and through
   The vorpal blade went snicker-snack!
He left it dead, and with its head
   He went galumphing back.

"And hast thou slain the Jabberwock?
   Come to my arms, my beamish boy!
Oh frabjous day! Calooh! Callay!"
   He chortled in his joy.

'Twas brillig, and the slithy toves
　　Did gyre and gimble in the wabe:
All mimsy were the borogoves,
　　And the mome raths outgrabe.

You can see in "Jabberwocky" that the writer uses a combination of real English words and made-up words. Also, he writes the poem in the same pattern as real English. The funny effect of this nonsense depends on it sounding as if it made sense.

Perhaps you have noticed in "Jabberwocky" that Lewis Carroll made up some of his nonsense words by combining two actual English words. "Mimsy," for instance is "miserable" and "flimsy" joined together; and "slithy" is a combination of "lithe" and "slimy."

Actually this idea of combining words is not such nonsense. Many of Carroll's nonsense words are used as real words today: "burble" is just one of them, "chortle" is another. Such words as "brunch" (from "breakfast" and "lunch"), "motel" (from "motor" plus "hotel"), and "smog" (from "smoke" and "fog"), were made up in the same way as Carroll made up his nonsense words. Can you think of any other words we use that are made up in this way?

Although nonsense language is fun, ordinarily language should make sense. If it didn't make sense, our written and spoken words would not communicate our

66

ideas and feelings to others. We can quote Lewis Carroll again to point out how necessary it is to use language in an exact way.

Humpty-Dumpty's proud statement doesn't fool Alice:

"When I use a word," Humpty-Dumpty said, in a rather scornful tone, "it means just what I *choose* it to mean—neither more nor less."

"The question is," said Alice, "whether you *can* make words mean so many different things."

Alice, of course, was bothered by the fact that Humpty-Dumpty used words as if they had no meaning other than those *he* wanted to give them. But words used that way have no meaning at all.

The real magic of words lies in the fact that they *can* bring *meaning* to us. With the help of these useful servants, men can understand so many things—and pass on that understanding. It may not be an exaggeration to say we owe the way we live today to the magic of words.

But words have two edges, and they can cut both ways. They may bring much that is good to us, but they can also hurt us, in spite of the rhyme that says:

Sticks and stones
Can break my bones
But names will never hurt me!

And, just as words can hurt, they can confuse problems instead of clearing them up—if we use words carelessly.

For there is both "good" and "bad" in the magic of words.

INDEX